ROBERT FROST

Warren Hope

GREENWICH EXCHANGE
LONDON

Greenwich Exchange, London

First published in Great Britain in 2004
Reprinted 2008
All rights reserved

Printed and bound by Q3 Digital/Litho, Loughborough
Tel: 01509 213456
Typesetting and layout by Albion Associates, London
Tel: 020 8852 4646
Cover design by December Publications, Belfast
Tel: 028 90286559

Cover: Picture of Robert Frost © Getty Images

Greenwich Exchange Website: www.greenex.co.uk

ISBN-13: 978-1-871551-70-9
ISBN-10: 1-871551-70-6

for Frank X. Smith

Contents

Chronology

1874 Born in San Francisco on 26th March, the first child of Isabelle Moodie and William Prescott Frost, Jr.

1876 Jeanie, Frost's sister, is born on 25th June.

1885 William Prescott Frost, Jr., dies of tuberculosis on 5th May.

1888 Entered Lawrence High School in Massachusetts where he pursues a college preparatory course of study.

1890 Frost's first published poem appears in the Lawrence High School *Bulletin* in April.

1891 Passes entrance exams for Harvard. Elected editor of the *Bulletin*.

1892 Graduates from Lawrence High School where he shares honours as Valedictorian with Elinor Miriam White, the girl, two years his senior, he would marry. Enters Dartmouth College, but leaves before the end of the term in December.

1894 Frost's 'My Butterfly: An Elegy' appears in *The Independent* on 8th November.

1895 Marries Elinor Miriam White on 19th December in Lawrence.

1896 Elliott, a son, born to the Frosts on 25th September.

1897 Enters Harvard as a freshman.

1898 Wins a scholarship through his academic performance. Withdraws from Harvard in March.

1899 Daughter Lesley born on 28th April. Sets up as a chicken farmer in Methuen, Massachusetts.

1900 Son Elliott dies of cholera on 8th July. Moves to farm in Derry, New Hampshire. Mother dies on 2nd November.

1901 William Prescott Frost, Frost's grandfather, dies, leaving an estate that provides Frost with an annual income and, eventually, ownership of the farm.

1906 Teaches at Pinkerton Academy. Publishes 'The Tuft of Flowers' in the *Derry Enterprise*.

1911 Teaches at the State Normal School. Moves family to Plymouth.

1912 Sails from Boston for England on 23rd August. Prepares manuscript of *A Boy's Will* in a rented cottage in Beaconsfield. Book accepted for publication by David Nutt and Company of London.

1913 Meets F.S. Flint at Harold Monro's Poetry Bookshop. Through Flint, meets Ezra Pound; through Pound, meets T.E. Hulme, Ford Madox Ford, W.B. Yeats, and others. *A Boy's Will* published.

1914 Moves to Dymock, Gloucestershire, to be near friends, Wilfred Gibson and Lascelles Abercrombie. *North of Boston* published by David Nutt and Company. First World War begins in August.

1915 Sails from Liverpool to New York on 13th February. *North of Boston* published by Holt in February. *A Boy's Will* published by Holt in April.

1916 *Mountain Interval* published by Holt.

1917   Teaches at Amherst College. Edward Thomas killed in France on 9th April.

1920   Frost commits Jeanie, his sister, to the state mental hospital in Augusta, Maine.

1923   *Selected Poems* published by Holt. *New Hampshire* published by Holt.

1924   Receives the Pulitzer Prize for *New Hampshire.*

1928   *West-Running Brook* published by Holt.

1930   *Collected Poems* published by Holt.

1931   Receives the Pulitzer Prize for *Collected Poems.*

1935   Frost meets Wallace Stevens in Key West, Florida. Stevens says, "You write on subjects." Frost says, "You write on bric-a-brac." Edwin Arlington Robinson dies in April.

1936   Named Charles Eliot Norton Professor of Poetry at Harvard. Becomes friend of Theodore Morrison and his wife, Kathleen. *A Further Range* published by Holt.

1937   Receives the Pulitzer Prize for *A Further Range.*

1938   Elinor Frost dies on 20th March. Frost moves into an apartment in Boston.

1939   Receives the Gold Medal from the National Institute of Arts and Letters. Enlarged *Collected Poems* published by Holt.

1940   Frost's son Carol commits suicide on 9th October.

1941   Buys a house in Cambridge, Massachusetts. Will spend the rest of his life there, with summers in Ripton, Vermont, and winters in South Miami, Florida.

1942 *A Witness Tree* published by Holt.

1943 Receives the Pulitzer Prize for *A Witness Tree*.

1947 T.S. Eliot surprises Frost by turning up at the door of his house in Cambridge for a visit. *Steeple Bush* published by Holt.

1949 *Complete Poems of Robert Frost 1949* published by Holt. Ezra Pound, then in Saint Elizabeth's mental hospital, is awarded the Bollingen Prize, to Frost's chagrin, for his *Pisan Cantos*.

1950 US Senate adopts a resolution to honour Frost on his birthday. The Korean War begins.

1953 Receives the Fellowship of the Academy of American Poets.

1957 Receives honorary Litt. D. degrees from Oxford and Cambridge while on a trip to England sponsored by the US Department of State.

1961 Takes part in the inauguration of President John F. Kennedy on 21st January.

1962 *In The Clearing* published by Holt. Goes to the Soviet Union as part of a cultural exchange programme. Meets the Soviet Premier, Nikita Khruschev.

1963 Dies 29th January.

Introduction

Late in life, Robert Frost lamented that his early poem 'Mending Wall' had been "spoiled" by its being "applied". Frost meant by this that the poem had been rendered unnecessarily limited because of political interpretations of it.

For instance, when Frost visited Jerusalem with his official biographer, Lawrance Thompson, a number of Israeli children asked for the famous poet's autograph. Jerusalem was then divided, and barbed wire and a concrete wall separated Frost and the children from what was then considered to be the Jordanian sector of the city. Frost told Thompson to select a single line from his works and write it down. Frost would then sign the paper for the children. Thompson wrote, "Something there is that doesn't love a wall," becoming guilty of spoiling 'Mending Wall' by applying its first line to a specific political situation.

Another example: Frost himself publicly read the poem when he was in Russia, then the Soviet Union, in 1962, when many people were critical of the East German government for erecting the Berlin Wall. Some of those attending the reading assumed Frost was making a political statement, attacking the wall in Berlin by reading his verses in Moscow. Frost disavowed any such intention. "I've had lots of adventures with that poem," he said. "People are frequently misunderstanding it or misinterpreting it. The secret of what it means, I keep."

The English poet James Reeves has done more than anyone else to help us get at the secret of what 'Mending Wall' means. He first pointed out that the poem is basically a riddle, a riddle that Frost wants his readers to solve even though he will not give the solution away to them. He wants them to work it out for themselves. The key to that riddle is in the poem's first line, the line Lawrance Thompson chose to write out in Jerusalem, "Something there is that doesn't love a wall."

This line of blank verse, of unrhymed iambic pentameter, opens with a traditional and acceptable variation of the poem's metre. It opens with a trochee, that is, an accented syllable followed by an unaccented one – *something,* rather than with an iamb, an unaccented syllable followed by an accented one. This inversion, this flipping of the weights of the line's first two syllables, serves to draw attention to the inversion of the line's word order. The normal word order of "There is something that doesn't love a wall" is inverted to put the emphasis on, to draw attention to, the word "Something". The reason for the poet drawing attention to the word in this way is to cause the reader to ask, "What is it? What is this something that doesn't love a wall?" It is this question that makes the poem a riddle, a riddle set by the poet for the reader to solve.

Another sign that this line poses the basic question of the poem is its repetition in line 35, but now with an emphatic action to define the something's lack of love for a wall, "Something there is that doesn't love a wall,/ That wants it down." Readers are here encouraged to ask what it is that wants the wall down.

The poem tells the story of a springtime ritual in Frost's native New England. Each spring, farmers walk on either side of stone walls to repair them by replacing stones that have come loose and fallen to the ground. Frost, the first-person narrator of the poem, describes this repair work as a game:

> Oh, just another kind of outdoor game,
> One on a side. It comes to little more:
> There where it is we do not need the wall:
> He is all pine and I am apple orchard.

That the wall is unnecessary only serves to add to the importance of the game, the ritual. If the wall were necessary – in order to keep the animals of each farmer from mingling, say – the farmers in repairing the wall would be merely fulfilling a practical obligation. By fixing a wall that does not need to exist they raise the fundamental question of why the wall is there at all. The poet jokingly urges his neighbour to recognize and agree to the wall's unnecessary quality:

> My apple trees will never get across
> And eat the cones under his pines, I tell him.

The neighbour does not respond with a joke but rather with a proverb, a piece of folk wisdom, rooted in custom, that through repetition has taken on the force of law, "He only says, 'Good fences make good neighbours'".

At this point in the poem, an odd thing happens. The reader in effect takes the neighbour's place. Frost confides in his readers a conversation he merely thought of having with the neighbour but did not really have. In a way, he gives his readers clues to the solution of the riddle that he kept from his neighbour. "I could say 'Elves' to him,/ But it's not elves exactly, and I'd rather/ He said it for himself."

At this point, attentive readers are in a position to solve the riddle and part company with the neighbour, to, as it were, leap over the wall or wriggle through a gap in it to join the poet. What it is that doesn't love a wall, that wants it down, is something that (1) causes the ground beneath the wall to swell, (2) spills boulders from the wall, (3) leaves gaps in the wall, and (4) has something to do with elves or, at least, with one specific elf, Jack Frost. Frost it is that doesn't love a wall, that wants it down, that annually tries to destroy it – the frost that thaws each spring, toppling stones, and Frost the poet who wants to use language in a way that binds people together rather than separating them.

Riddles, jokes, spells, puns, games, the playful and magical use of language is the poetic use of language. It does not lay down the law with a single, blunt, rock-like meaning the way the neighbour's unquestioned proverb does. Instead, it teases people into discovering meanings for themselves. Those readers who recognise the riddle in this poem and solve it, temporarily become Frost, the poet that doesn't love a wall, temporarily become the author of the poem, the source of its meaning. Readers who 'spoil' the poem by 'applying' it, who try to limit its meaning to a specific time, place, or political situation, become the neighbour, relying on the repetition of a single meaning that is not their own discovery but merely handed down from someone else:

> I see him there,
> Bringing a stone grasped firmly by the top
> In each hand, like an old-stone savage armed.
> He moved in darkness as it seemed to me,
> Not of woods only and the shade of trees.
> He will not go behind his father's saying,
> And he likes having thought of it so well
> He says again, "Good fences make good neighbors."

This early and popular poem by Frost, popular to some extent because it has been misunderstood, makes clear that there are at least two Robert Frosts. First, there is the playful and private poet who actually wrote 'Mending Wall'. Second, there is the public figure who performed the poem, allowing it to be spoiled by being applied while keeping to himself the secret of what it meant. In other words, Robert Frost is at once the narrator of 'Mending Wall' and the neighbour, two contradictory characters simultaneously bound together and kept separate by the ethereal wall of language. As Jay Parini, one of Frost's biographers, reports, Frost himself said he was at once a wall-builder and a wall-destroyer.

1

A Boy's Will

As if to demonstrate the contradictory nature of Robert Frost's character, he was born in San Francisco, California, on 26th March 1874, about as far away from the New England with which he was to become permanently identified, as it was possible to go and remain in the United States; and he was named Robert Lee by his father, in honour of the Confederate general who opposed the Union Army in the American Civil War, the army supported by the vast majority of New Englanders. Frost's place of birth and name marked him as something of an odd man out and a rebel from the start.

The two parts of Frost's contradictory nature – the romantic and the realist, the man of faith and the devout sceptic, the private person and the public persona – seem to align with his parents, Isabelle Moodie and William Prescott Frost, Jr. She was born in Scotland, and emigrated to the United States at the age of 12 to be raised by an uncle in Columbus, Ohio. He was the only child of an old New England family, born in Kingston, New Hampshire, raised in Lawrence, Massachusetts, a Phi Beta Kappa graduate of Harvard, and six years younger than his wife. They met when both were teachers at an academy in Lewistown, Pennsylvania. An early letter William Prescott Frost, Jr. wrote to Isabelle Moodie shows that his lack of religion already served as a joking difference, if not a source of contention, between them. She was a Swedenborgian who also loved to tell stories of elves and fairies, and in fact wrote verses and stories. He was a hard-headed journalist with a passion for politics. In San Francisco, the father was city editor of the *Daily Evening Post,* a paper edited by Henry George, the social reformer whose theory of a 'single tax' sought economic justice by taxing only the ownership of land. In time, Frost's mother wrote book reviews and poems that were published in the paper. Here in miniature are the poles of the mature Frost's personality, the private and the public life, poetry and politics, the writer and the performer.

The differences between Frost's parents were heightened by a kind of instability. When Frost was two, his mother, then pregnant with his sister, Jeanie, took him across the country to live with his father's parents in Lawrence, Massachusetts. Jeanie was born there. The mother then took the children to her relatives in Ohio. She seems to have left her husband because of his drinking and gambling. When she eventually returned to San Francisco and her husband, she took with her her own mother and sister, and a friend of her mother's who became known to the children as Aunt Blanche. This predominantly female horde frequently moved from place to place in San Francisco. The father was soon diagnosed with tuberculosis, the disease that killed him in 1885 when Frost was 11 years old, an event that sent the family across the country again to be geographically close to the Frost family and the support they could provide.

The year before the death of William Prescott Frost, Jr., he had quit his job on the newspaper to run for the office of city tax collector on the Democratic ticket. Robert Frost, a boy of ten, worked enthusiastically with his father on this political campaign. Defeated at the polls, the father, in poor health and unemployed, became despondent. The young poet might well have associated the father's death with this political defeat. In his absence, the father – something of an athlete as well as a journalist and politician, a drinker and a gambler – took on a mythic quality for the poet, a quality possibly conveyed through a remembered storm in 'Once by the Pacific', the ocean in which the father swam far out from shore while the boy watched in fear:

> The clouds were low and hairy in the skies,
> Like locks blown forward in the gleam of eyes.

Although the mother could rely on her husband's family, she struggled to be independent of them and tried to support her children on her own by teaching school. She seems to have been so gentle and kind that she had difficulty controlling classes, especially classes of older boys. Frost's earliest experiences as a teacher seem to have come about by his taking over classes that gave his mother trouble. In fact, for a time, Frost seems to have tried to follow in the footsteps of his parents by alternating work as a teacher with work as a journalist.

He had been a very good student, and obtained an excellent classical education from the Lawrence High School in Massachusetts. In 1890, he began to publish poems in the school magazine; eventually, he became the editor of the magazine which was entitled the *Bulletin*. He finished each year at the head of his class and passed entrance examinations for Harvard College. More important than any of these academic achievements, however, was his meeting and falling in love with a slightly older classmate, Elinor Miriam White. She was an unconventional girl, and a good student, who early became a recipient of – as well as the subject of – many of Frost's early poems. As if to establish her relationship to his poetry, in 1892 he gave her a copy of Emily Dickinson's *Poems,* first published two years earlier. Frost and Elinor became secretly engaged to be married that year, exchanging rings in a private ceremony.

Frost was dependent on his father's parents to finance his education. They blamed the undergraduate life of Harvard men in Boston for the habits – the drinking, the gambling, and the free thinking – that, in their view, had marred their son's life. As a result, Frost went to Dartmouth and always displayed his lingering resentment by pointing out that Dartmouth's fees were lower than those of Harvard, suggesting that meanness prompted his grandfather's decision. It could well have been the enforced separation from Elinor, who had gone away to St Lawrence University in New York state, that made Frost so unhappy, bored, and restless at Dartmouth that he left in December without completing a single semester. He worked at a variety of jobs – as a labourer in local mills, as a teacher, as a journalist – while demanding that Elinor quit college to marry him. She refused.

In 1894, when Frost was 20, a magazine called *The Independent* accepted his poem 'My Butterfly: An Elegy', for publication, and agreed to pay him $15.00. As a result, he began a continuing correspondence with the magazine's literary editor, Susan Hayes Ward. In that same year, he issued at his own expense a small book entitled *Twilight* in an edition of two copies, one for himself and one for Elinor. He took the book, which consisted of five poems, with him to St Lawrence University to present Elinor with her copy, perhaps with the hope that doing so would persuade her to leave school and marry him. In any case, he was exceedingly disappointed by her reaction to the gift. The result was a symbolic, nightmarish, and perhaps suicidal episode. He destroyed his copy of *Twilight,* and then left home without a word to anyone.

His intent seems to have been to go to the Dismal Swamp, where Virginia runs into North Carolina. The name of this swamp no doubt represents Frost's state of mind, and was perhaps the name of the place where he had chosen to die. Virginia was Robert E. Lee's home state, and during the Civil War Frost's father had left Harvard with the intention of serving in Lee's Army of Virginia. Frost's flight to the Dismal Swamp can be seen as an unconscious attempt on his part to join his father's ghost. He travelled by boat and train, and then hiked, walking at night in the swamp for miles. In time, he came across boatmen who took him through the swamp, perhaps saving his life. He tried to travel home by hopping freight trains, but he eventually wrote to his mother and asked for the money to buy a ticket home. He arrived in Lawrence at the end of November. One year later, on 19th December 1895, he married Elinor White. A Swedenborgian pastor conducted the ceremony.

'My Butterfly: An Elegy' is the only poem from the self-published volume *Twilight* that appeared in Frost's first book, *A Boy's Will,* published in England in 1913, 19 years after the poem was written. The poem is said to commemorate Frost's discovery of a dead butterfly in a window of his room at Dartmouth College. There can be little doubt that Frost also wrote the poem as a way of considering his relationship with Elinor. It has some traits of his mature work – accurate depiction of nature that conveys a mood and an intricate use of form based on rhymes and varying line lengths:

> The gray grass is scarce dappled with the snow;
> Its two banks have not shut upon the river;
> But it is long ago –
> It seems forever –
> Since first I saw thee glance.

That this poem was published in a national magazine while Frost was literally tramping through the Dismal Swamp suggests that if something symbolically died in that swamp, something was born there too:

> Then when I was distraught
> And could not speak,
> Sidelong, full on my cheek,
> What should that reckless zephyr fling
> But the wild touch of thy dye-dusty wing!

I found that wing broken today!
For thou art dead, I said,
And the strange birds say.
I found it with the withered leaves
Under the eaves.

There might be a touch of madness in that line, "And the strange birds say". It seems to spring unbidden from the poet's pen. Mad or not, the gleam of poetry is certainly in it.

✧　✧　✧　✧

Frost's first child, a son, Elliott, was born on 25th September 1896. This additional responsibility encouraged him to pursue a more settled way of life. He borrowed money from his grandfather and entered Harvard College as a freshman in the fall of 1897. Elinor, Elliott, and Elinor's mother joined him in Cambridge, establishing a household in a rented apartment. He won a scholarship through the excellence of his academic work, and returned to Harvard the following year. Elinor, pregnant again, stayed in Lawrence. Frost travelled back and forth between Cambridge and Lawrence to visit his family and to teach night classes at a school owned and operated by his mother. In the spring of 1899, Frost left Harvard and took a step that did not follow in the footsteps of either of his parents: he set up as a chicken farmer with the financial help of his grandfather. Lesley, a daughter, was born on 28th April 1899.

Frost and his wife were overwhelmed by the death of their son in the summer of 1900. Elinor became deeply depressed and seemed completely helpless to throw off her grief. Frost suffered symptoms that made him suspect that he, like his father, had tuberculosis. Later that same year, Frost's mother died of cancer. What seems to have been the family's saving grace was their move to a farm in Derry, New Hampshire. Elinor took the initiative to go and convince Frost's grandfather to purchase the farm for their use. He did so, and also stipulated in his will that Frost would own the farm outright after occupying it for ten years. In addition, the grandfather left both Frost and his sister annual cash incomes.

The seasons on the farm in Derry appeared to Frost to mirror his mental states. When spring arrived, he felt physically and mentally well again, and happy. He had also been writing poems at night. One of these, 'Storm Fear', eventually gathered in *A Boy's Will,* commemorates that winter:

> I count our strength,
> Two and a child,
> Those of us not asleep subdued to mark
> How the cold creeps as the fire dies at length –
> How drifts are piled,
> Dooryard and road ungraded,
> Till even the comforting barn grows far away,
> And my heart owns a doubt
> Whether 'tis in us to arise with day
> And save ourselves unaided.

For Frost, this doubt about the ability of his family to rise unaided – and the fact of their rising, – in the morning after a stormy night, in the spring after a long, hard winter, and in their ability to endure the deaths of a son and a mother – led to a lack of doubt in the existence of God. It was Elinor who found it impossible to reconcile the death of Elliott with the existence of God. The question of religious faith and the question of whether Frost should seek solitude (the Dismal Swamp) or company (the Derry farm) dominate the structure and content of *A Boy's Will.*

Frost never was much of a farmer. When his grandfather bought the farm for him, he insisted that two old friends live on the farm to help with the work of it. Their attitude towards work or what might best be called chores was one of the things on which Frost and Elinor found complete agreement. He would neglect the farm and she would neglect the house so they could take long walks, trying to identify trees, flowers, and birds, or sit indoors where he would read great gobs of poems or stories to her. It is clear that they both thought of this as a 'poetic' existence, and he certainly did write a lot, up alone late at night. In time, he let the pretence that he was a farmer go, and returned to teaching.

If having the farm to work and live on provided the Frosts with one kind of salvation, the eventual sale of the farm provided another kind. The proceeds of that sale funded the trip to England that served to establish his reputation as a poet.

Frost never submitted a book-length manuscript of poems to any American publisher. He sent very few poems to editors of American magazines. Some of his poems appeared in *The Independent* and he continued to correspond with and visit its literary editor, Susan Hayes Ward. He seems to have relied on her as a tie to the literary world. 'Into My Own', the poem that opened *A Boy's Will,* in form a variation on a Shakespearean sonnet, ends with these lines, giving the sense that Frost had found himself as a poet or, at least, had discovered a self that would allow him to continue as a poet, through his temporary disappearance in the Dismal Swamp:

> I do not see why I should e'er turn back,
> Or those should not set forth upon my track
> To overtake me, who should miss me here
> And long to know if still I held them dear.
>
> They would not find me changed from him they knew –
> Only more sure of all I thought was true.

On 23rd August 1912, Frost and Elinor and their three children, Lesley, Carol, a son, and Marjorie set sail for England from Boston. Frost's intention was to launch his career as a poet with the sailing of that ship. Elinor again expressed her idea of the poetic life by saying they chose England because she wanted to live "under thatch".

Later, Frost liked to say he had taken the manuscripts of his first three books of poems with him to England. No doubt this was an exaggeration, but he certainly did take a mass of poems with him and planned to revise them and arrange them into volumes. Within months of his arrival in England, once the family had settled into a rented cottage in suburban Beaconsfield, Buckinghamshire, Frost prepared the manuscript of *A Boy's Will* and submitted it to David Nutt and Company, a London publisher. Before the end of 1912, it had been accepted for publication.

A Boy's Will is a collection of 30 poems, most of them short and lyrical. Frost was not content to let these poems go as a collection of individual lyrics, arranged in the order of their composition, perhaps. Instead, probably taking a page from the practice of W.B. Yeats, a poet he read and admired, he arranged the poems on the basis of theme and imagery so that the lyrics carried an implied narrative. He went so far as to add glosses that insisted on this narrative, a kind of narrative of maturation tied to the seasons of the year. The volume also metaphorically explores Frost's relationship with his wife.

'My November Guest', clearly identifying the season as that of "dark days of autumn rain", states that Elinor – described by the poet as "my Sorrow" – thinks these days are the most beautiful and is annoyed that the poet does not share her view. He does not protest, but rather, in the conclusion of an almost perfect lyric, wittily states why he remains silent in the face of her annoyance:

> Not yesterday I learned to know
> The love of bare November days
> Before the coming of the snow,
> But it were vain to tell her so,
> And they are better for her praise.

'My November Guest' is one of the kinds of poems Frost would continue to write from time to time throughout his long life – love poems marked by musicality, wit, strong feeling, and clarity of statement. This first book contained other poems that, in retrospect, seem typical of the Frost who became famous – the epigrammatic 'In Neglect', the conversational 'Mowing', and 'The Tuft of Flowers', a narrative of discovery, a narrative with a philosophical point, are examples.

The story of Frost's entrance into literary society is well known. He visited Harold Monro's recently opened Poetry Bookshop in Kensington. There F.S. Flint, one of the Imagists, noticed Frost's shoes, recognised them as American, and struck up a conversation. One consequence of this new acquaint-anceship was for Frost to meet Ezra Pound. Pound was then a one-man volunteer public relations firm for the arts in general and for poetry in particular. When *A Boy's Will* first appeared in April of 1913, Pound praised it in *Poetry: A Magazine of Verse,* the highly influential Chicago-based journal. Pound also introduced Frost to a large number of poets and writers, including T.E. Hulme, Ford Madox Ford, and William Butler Yeats. Pound and Frost were very different types, however, and Frost eventually found more congenial literary company among those who became known as the Georgian poets, Wilfred Gibson, Lascelles Abercrombie, W.H. Davies, and Ralph Hodgson. It was Ralph Hodgson who introduced Frost to the man who was to become his best and closest friend in England, Edward Thomas, who was killed in France in 1917 during the First World War.

Frost's ambition took on a very specific shape. He was not content to be well regarded by literary people. His aim was to get beyond that small and rather precious circle to reach ordinary readers. His reason for wishing to do so is clear – he wanted to make a living from poetry without the need to do any other kind of work. The annual income from his grandfather's estate and the sales achieved by some of the popular poets of the day made this a realistic ambition.

One of the poems in *A Boy's Will* that pointed the way for Frost's future was 'A Tuft of Flowers'. It's a first-person narrative, the narrator identifiable with the poet, consisting of 20 couplets, the simplest of rhyme schemes. The language is casual, conversational, but playful, and identifies the speaker as a working man, a farmer or, at least, an agricultural worker:

> I went to turn the grass once after one
> Who mowed it in the dew before the sun.

The narrator, faced with this evidence of having been preceded by a fellow worker, nonetheless has a philosophical predisposition to insist on the aloneness, the solitariness, and therefore the individualism of humanity. "All must be" alone, he said "within" his "heart,"/ "Whether they work together or apart."

The story of this poem is the story of a little conversion, of a turning away, a change of heart. What leads the speaker to this conversion is a butterfly – perhaps the butterfly that will eventually become the subject of an elegy – who directs the speaker's attention to:

> a tall tuft of flowers beside a brook,

> A leaping tongue of bloom the scythe has spared
> Beside a reedy brook the scythe had bared.

> The mower in the dew had loved them thus,
> By leaving them to flourish, not for us,

> Nor yet to draw one thought of ours to him,
> But from sheer morning gladness at the brim.

It is hard to suppress the notion that this tuft of flowers metaphorically represents poems, things that are left to flourish not for readers, nor yet to draw attention to the poet, but from an unconscious impulse, a kind of joy that might be considered the equivalent of "sheer morning gladness". Still, the flowers make a kind of sense, can be read, offer "a message from the dawn":

> "Men work together," I told him from the heart,
> "Whether they work together or apart."

In a way, this poem celebrates Frost's shift from a poet who might simply achieve critical acclaim by remaining alone and giving voice within his own heart to a philosophy that insists on solitude, aloofness, to a poet who speaks from the heart to another, giving voice to a communal philosophy. The use of a conversational narrative to record the discovery of this shift seems to forecast the dominant form of the poems in his second book, the book that made him a popular poet, *North of Boston.*

2

North of Boston

Gertrude Stein said Ezra Pound was "a village explainer" – and that that was all very well if you were a village. It is likely that Pound mistook Frost for a village; Frost often liked to disguise himself as one anyway. The result was a tense and awkward relationship.

They were very different types. Pound as an aesthete and expatriate can be seen to have taken the path of Henry James, a path that at least suggested and perhaps lamented that America was hostile to, lethal for, 'artists'. Frost, on the other hand, sailed to England with the intention of staying there temporarily to concentrate on writing so that he could establish himself in America. Pound eventually spoke on Rome radio in praise of the Axis powers; Frost eventually took part in the inauguration of a President of the United States. In literary matters, Pound founded the Imagist movement and seems to have tried to bully Frost into becoming an Imagist or, at least, a *vers librist*, a writer of free verse. Frost in time compared writing poetry without metre and rhyme to playing tennis with the net down.

Despite these differences, there is no doubt that Pound and Frost helped each other. Pound's praise of Frost's first two books and the resulting publication of Frost's poems in *Poetry: A Magazine of Verse,* based in Chicago, did much to establish Frost's reputation and launch his career, as if it were a boat. Frost eventually did much to have Pound released from St Elizabeth's hospital for the insane in Washington, DC, where he had been kept on the grounds that he was not competent to stand trial for treason. Frost complained that Pound's praise might do as much harm as good. Pound complained that Frost had taken his time about securing his release. They were both complainers.

It would be a mistake, however, to think of Pound as the avant-garde experimentalist and of Frost as the old-fashioned upholder of tradition, as poetic opposites. The taste and practice of both of them were to a large extent shaped by the poetry of the 1890s, including, but not limited to, the poetry of W.B. Yeats. Both started out writing poems that used 'thee' and 'thy', inverted the normal order of words for the sake of the metre or rhyme, relied on a blatantly artificial 'poetic' language, and seemed to put Form with a capital 'F' over substance. Both in their different ways became dissatisfied with these practices and, to a greater or lesser extent, left them behind.

Pound's way was the way of the aesthete, a neo-pagan way that has its roots in the 'art for art's sake' movement of the decadent 1890s. Frost's way was the way of the storyteller, a quasi-Christian way with its roots in the Wordsworthian ideal of the poet as 'a man speaking to men'. Both were ambitious. Pound's ambition led him to write *The Cantos,* an attempt at a modern epic that consists of a collection of fragments, the most powerful and moving of which often echo the poetic practice of the nineteenth century:

> What thou lov'st well remains, the rest is dross;
> What thou lov'st well is thy true heritage.

Frost's ambition led him to publish too much, offering the public stretches of dullness and unfunny light verse. Frost's most powerful lines and passages, however, are completely free of the poetic practice of the nineteenth century:

I cannot rub the strangeness from my sight
I got from looking through a pane of glass
I skimmed this morning from the drinking trough.

In retrospect, Frost is closer than Pound to the central movement in English poetry of the twentieth century, the movement from Form with a capital 'F' to form with a lower case 'f', the movement from false, artificial 'poetic' diction to the conversational but magical speech of ordinary life. Frost's friend, Edward Thomas, in his review of *North of Boston,* clearly isolated Frost's peculiar contribution to the movement in English poetry that began shortly before the First World War:

> This is one of the most revolutionary books of modern times, but one of the quietest and least aggressive. It speaks, and it is poetry ... These poems are revolutionary because they lack the exaggeration of rhetoric, and even at first sight appear to lack the poetic intensity of which rhetoric is an imitation ... They succeed in being plain though not mean, in reminding us of poetry without being falsely 'poetical'.

Frost is sometimes thought of as hostile to theorising about poetry. He was not. He liked to go to visit Pound's friend T.E. Hulme in London to discuss theories of language and poetry. Wilfred Gibson, the Georgian poet, pictures Frost indulging in monologues late at night, holding a small audience of fellow poets captive with his talk. He had what he took to be a new and original definition of the sentence that he wrote letters to friends about and discussed at length with Edward Thomas. He defined the sentence as a sound with a sense of its own apart from the meanings of the words that make it up. He offered as an example statements overheard through a closed door in which the individual words could not be discerned. This idea of the sentence can be seen, or rather heard, at work in Frost's second book, *North of Boston,* published by David

Nutt and Company in London just months before the outbreak of the First World War, a war that would take the lives of T.E. Hulme, Edward Thomas, and a whole generation of British and European youth, a war that would leave the race wary of rhetoric.

North of Boston (the title is said to have been taken from a realtor's ad in a Boston newspaper) is a very different book from *A Boy's Will*. The first book, with its attempt to decide between solitude and society was, in a way, self-involved and so, in a way, small and brittle, consisting of 30 short lyrics. One result is that Frost's voice in that first book is less distinctive, less self-assured than it is in the second:

> Thou didst not know, who tottered, wandering on high,
> That fate had made thee for the pleasure of the wind,
> With those great careless wings,
> Nor yet did I.

These lines are unexceptionable but generic and might have been written by any number of Frost's contemporaries. Turning from them to the first line of the first poem in *North of Boston* produces something of a shock, a slight shock, but a shock all the same:

> Something there is that doesn't love a wall.

North of Boston opens with 'Mending Wall', a poem set on a New England farm on a day in spring, and closes with 'Good Hours', a brief poem that serves as a kind of coda for the volume, set in a New England village at night in winter. Bound between these are the volume's most typical poems, long poems that use the techniques of the storyteller and the dramatist to capture and set down the speech of the people in Frost's part of the world.

The reader becomes an eavesdropper on gossip:

> Mary sat musing on the lamp-flame at the table
> Waiting for Warren.

is the opening sentence of 'The Death of the Hired Man', a poem of 167 lines of blank verse, the vast majority of which are spoken by the married couple, Mary and Warren, who are faced with the return of Silas, an old man Warren had formerly hired, but no longer wanted on the farm. The narrator merely serves to set the stage on which Mary and Warren speak, or intervenes briefly to heighten the language with lyricism:

> Part of a moon was falling down the west,
> Dragging the whole sky with it to the hills.
> Its light poured softly in her lap. She saw it
> And spread her apron to it. She put out her hand
> Among the harp like morning-glory strings,
> Taut with the dew from garden bed to eaves,
> As if she played unheard some tenderness
> That wrought on him beside her in the night.
> "Warren," she said, "he has come home to die:
> You needn't be afraid he'll leave you this time."

Just as in 'A Tuft of Flowers' and 'Mending Wall', Frost in this poem uses conversational language to probe definitions that are basic to humanity's life on a mud ball spinning through infinite space. Here the word to be defined is "home". The male character, Warren, offers what has become a well-known and often quoted definition:

> "Home is the place where, when you have to go there,
> They have to take you in."

In context, this definition probably has an edge of bitterness and mockery to it, the speaker of it not wishing to feel obliged to take the hired man in. Frost gives Mary, the wife, the female character, the last word on this subject:

" … I should have called it
Something you somehow haven't to deserve."

It is typical of Frost's fate that the more epigrammatic but less generous definition is the one that is most often remembered. Still, for any lines to be 'lodged' where they will be difficult to get rid of is, as Frost said, the height of ambition.

Frost was a serious student of classical languages and literatures – the literatures of Greece and Rome. The early poem 'My Butterfuly', written when Frost was 20, already shows an indebtedness to Catullus, a Roman poet Frost is on record as ranking very high. The narrative poems in *North of Boston* owe something to the eclogues of Virgil, but also to the moving objectivity of the Greek dramatists, especially Sophocles. Although Frost never reaches the emotion-wrenching heights of the Greek tragedians, he comes closest to them in 'Home Burial'.

Elliott Baker, the novelist and memoirist, reports that when he asked Frost to read 'Home Burial' for possible use on television, Frost rejected the idea, saying the poem was "too sad." Lawrance Thompson, Frost's official biographer, who attended hundreds of Frost's public readings, reports that Frost never read 'Home Burial' in public. The probable reason is that the poem is not only sad but also touches closely one of the saddest events in Frost's own life, the death of his first child, Elliott, and the effect of that death on his wife and their marriage.

Many of the poems in *North of Boston* focus on the differences between men and women, the differences in their outlooks and in their uses of language. 'Home Burial' explores the ways men and women grieve.

The poem is not, of course, a piece of autobiography, an accurate description of the Frosts' reaction to the death of their first child. Instead, Frost achieved some distance from the event and its aftermath, some objectivity, by changing some details. In the poem, for instance, Amy and her unnamed husband live in the husband's family's home, a home that includes the burial ground where the father buried the son while the wife looked on. Although Elliott Frost was buried at the Frost family home in Lawrence, Massachusetts, Frost and his wife lived on a chicken farm in Methuen, Massachusetts, when the boy died of cholera. It could well have been that Elinor was moved to approach Frost's grandfather and arrange for the purchase of the farm in Derry, New Hampshire, because of her reaction to Elliott's death and her wish to get away from the scene of it. To the extent that 'Home Burial' can be said to have a plot, it is that Amy wishes to leave the house, to separate herself from the memory of her husband burying their son and then, as she thinks, simply going on with the business of life, while the husband tries to convince her to stay. The plot reaches its climax when the husband breaks a taboo by speaking of the dead child:

" ... it is not the stones,
But the child's mound – "

"Don't, don't, don't, don't," she cried.

She withdrew, shrinking from beneath his arm
That rested on the banister, and slid downstairs;
And turned on him with such a daunting look,
He said twice over before he knew himself:
"Can't a man speak of his own child he's lost?"

"Not you! – Oh, where's my hat? Oh, I don't need it!
I must get out of here. I must get air –
I don't know rightly whether any man can."

There is a hint of the husband's willingness to use force, violence, to keep his wife at home in this poem. It is present in the line, "She withdrew, shrinking from beneath his arm," and becomes overt in the poem's last line, a line spoken by the husband, "I'll follow and bring you back by force. I *will*! " Frost himself had a violent streak in him. When his mother had difficulties with unruly high school boys, Frost took over the class and caned the boys, no doubt exacting revenge for the boys' treatment of his mother as well as establishing control over the class. The boys got their own back by later beating Frost away from the school. For a time, Frost's mother supplemented her income as a teacher by taking in boarders. Frost was once fined for punching a boarder. Frost's destruction of his copy of the booklet *Twilight* and his quasi-suicidal flight to the Dismal Swamp in the face of what seemed to him Elinor's indifference to him, his love for her, and his work, no doubt represent the turning against himself of violent feelings aimed at Elinor. There is also the story of Frost, armed with a revolver, waking his daughter Lesley in the night and asking her to choose between him and her mother because they could not both survive the night. It is not surprising that Frost, for all his showmanship and love of performance, for all his willingness to please audiences and people who could further his reputation, could never bring himself to read 'Home Burial' in public.

The differences between Amy and her husband rest on the ability to understand the poetic use of language. As Elliott Baker has recorded, Frost used to teach classes and audiences that "Poetry provides the one permissible way of saying one thing and meaning another." But he knew the race was given to indulging in the practice on other occasions, for self-protective reasons or, as he said, through "diffidence". In 'The Death of the Hired Man', Mary urges Warren to go along with Silas' pretence that he has plans to work on the farm even though he is clearly dying. These plans for the future she takes to be regrets for the past, and she wants her husband to see them that way, too. In 'Home Burial', the husband's willingness to dig the child's grave and his reaction to it are misunderstood by Amy:

> "I can repeat the very words you were saying:
> 'Three foggy mornings and one rainy day
> Will rot the best birch fence a man can build.'
> "Think of it, talk like that at such a time!
> What had how long it takes a birch to rot
> To do with what was in the darkened parlor?"

Amy, in her grief and anger, lacked the patience and understanding to seriously consider the question of what talk of a rotting birch fence had to do with the dead child in the parlour. The husband was not making conversation about birch fences so much as raising a poetic lamentation that nothing in this world lasts for long. The married couple in 'Home Burial' is at odds because the male represents the indirect expression of emotion and the female represents the direct expression of it. The result is misunderstanding, the wish to flee, and the potential for violence.

North of Boston opens with spring and closes with winter, but the content arranged between these seasonal poles is varied. If Frost is at his best in sad, serious poems, he is also very good in whimsical ones, such as 'The Mountain'. In this poem, as in 'Mending Wall', Frost uses a first-person narrator, making the poem more personal, more subjective than 'The Death of the Hired Man' and 'Home Burial'. In 'The Mountain', the narrator sleeps near a mountain and, on waking, meets a man, a local, and asks him about the mountain and the town. The narrative opens with a striking statement: "The mountain held the town as in a shadow." The narrator's willingness to stop the man he meets is expressed in joking terms:

> And there I met a man who moved so slow
> With white-faced oxen, in a heavy cart,
> It seemed no harm to stop him altogether.

The stranger, the narrator, is interested in the mountain, thinks of climbing it another day, and asks the local man about it. The local, in the end almost a mythical figure, knows about the mountain mostly by hearsay, and offers familiarity as his reason for never having climbed it:

> "I've always meant to go
> And look myself, but you know how it is:
> It doesn't seem so much to climb a mountain
> You've worked around the foot of all your life."

Still, the man with the oxen is able to tell the visitor of one of the rumoured attractions of the mountain's top:

> "There's a brook
> That starts up on it somewhere – I've heard say
> Right on the top, tip-top – a curious thing.
> But what would interest you about the brook,
> It's always cold in summer, warm in winter.
> One of the great sights going is to see
> It steam in winter like an ox's breath,
> Until the bushes all along its banks
> Are inch-deep with the frosty spines and bristles –
> You know the kind. Then let the sun shine on it!"

This depiction of the brook haunts the conversation between the two men. Towards the poem's end, the stranger asks about it again: "Warm in December, cold in June, you say?" The man with the oxen responds with an explanation that might serve as a statement of Frost's poetic creed:

> "I don't suppose the water's changed at all.
> You and I know enough to know it's warm
> Compared with cold, and cold compared with warm.
> But all the fun's in how you say a thing."

The repetition of the word "warm" at the end of two lines of blank verse, of unrhymed iambic pentameter, is part of the fun of how this thing is said.

Another poem with a first-person narrator in *North of Boston is* 'The Wood-pile'. Unlike most of the poems in the book, this one is not a dialogue. Instead, it is similar to 'A Tuft of Flowers' in that the narrator reports on a discovery he makes while walking outdoors. This walk is clearly purposeless in that the narrator starts by thinking to turn back and then deciding to go on. The scene of the walk is a "frozen swamp" and so might represent Frost's flight to the Dismal Swamp, a flight from which he returned willing to live and with an increased dedication to being a poet.

At first, the poem appears to be as purposeless as the walk described. Once the narrator decides to proceed, he admits to being lost and defines his location in this way: "I was just far from home." In this condition, the narrator notices a bird who seems to give him a sense of direction. The bird leads him to the wood-pile and then disappears from sight and from the poem. The wood-pile represents something made and measured, the handiwork of humanity that had once apparently been accomplished for a purpose. The pile has been there a long time, vegetation has grown on it, and part of it is about to fall so that it will lose its shape. Frost tries to explain the presence of the wood-pile:

> I thought that only
> Someone who lived in turning to fresh tasks
> Could so forget his handiwork on which
> He spent himself, the labor of his ax,
> And leave it there far from a useful fireplace
> To warm the frozen swamp as best it could
> With the slow smokeless burning of decay.

Frost, who was fond of saying one thing in terms of another, no doubt saw his poems as neat and measured stacks of language that he left to warm the frozen swamp of the world as best they could.

3

Mountain Interval

Frost said *North of Boston* was not written as a book, but rather as a collection of individual pieces that, in time, gathered themselves into a book. He no doubt made this point because readers and reviewers were struck by the relative uniformity of the book's tone, despite its variations in form, content, and even point of view. This tone did seem to characterise people from a single section of the United States, New England in general, and rural New Hampshire and Vermont in particular. It was Frost's ability to depict New Englanders that drew his work to the notice of Mrs Henry Holt, the wife of the publisher. She wrote Frost a fan letter, and eventually Henry Holt became Frost's publisher, arranging with David Nutt of London to bring out first *North of Boston* and then *A Boy's Will* in the United States. When Frost received word that these arrangements had been made, he announced to his family that they could go home. The stay in England had served its purpose. He borrowed money from friends and sailed for New York from Liverpool on 13th February 1915, about seven months after the outbreak of the First World War. Holt had published *North of Boston* while Frost was crossing the Atlantic. On landing, he stayed in New York to visit his publishers and literary people while his family went on to New Hampshire.

In retrospect, Frost has the look of being both a late bloomer and an overnight success. He made something like a triumphal march through America's literary world, not only in New York but also in Boston, on his return from England. 'The Death of the Hired Man' had recently appeared in *The New Republic* along with a favourable review of *North of Boston* by Amy Lowell. The homecoming has the aspect of a premeditated, coordinated public relations campaign and the result was that both of Frost's books sold remarkably well. On the other hand, Frost was almost 39 years old when he stepped from the ship to the dock in New York. It was not for nothing that he always claimed a poet will hit his stride by the age of 40 or not at all.

Frost's reception shows that he was not originally neglected because of America's Philistinism as Pound had contended at Frost's urging, although it is certainly true that American editors and critics were in part willing to praise and publish him because he had been praised and published in England. Instead, it seems to be the case that although Frost was relatively precocious as a poet, writing publishable work as a high school boy, he needed years of experience of various kinds, years of reading, years of writing, years of farming, years of loving and grieving, as well as some years of financial independence far from his native New England, mixing with and talking to other poets and writers, in order to write work that was completely his own. *North of Boston* represented the culmination of that period, and pointed the way for him to continue with the publication of *Mountain Interval* in 1916, the year after his return from England.

Mountain Interval contains two of Frost's most famous poems, 'The Road Not Taken' and 'Birches'. 'The Road Not Taken' has entered the language, in the sense that it is now quoted, or misquoted, at least in part, in conversation by people who might not even be aware they are quoting a poem by Robert Frost. These words seem to encapsulate the experience of many of us and so serve as a kind of conversational shorthand:

Two roads diverged in a wood, and I –
I took the one less traveled by,
And that has made all the difference.

The second of these lines is often merged with the title of the poem to become "The road less traveled by". In a television commercial for Subaru, for instance, a male voice announces: "Just a reminder: the road less traveled by is probably unpaved" and goes on to praise the virtues of a Subaru off-road vehicle. For a poem to take on such uses is a testament to its popularity. This poem has been memorised by school children and written about by high school and college students. What seems to make the poem so popular is a simplification – or even an oversimplification – of it.

The poem is taken to represent a call for nonconformity and individualism, as if the poem were a kind of rhymed equivalent of Thoreau's "different drummer". And it is certainly the case that there is a strong element of this sense in the poem's three concluding lines, those memorable lines cited above that can be heard repeated in conversation.

What this emphasis on the concluding lines does is to diminish the point of the poem's title and the overt statement that the two roads had enjoyed or suffered more or less the same amount of traffic:

Though as for that, the passing there
Had worn them really about the same,

And both that morning equally lay
In leaves no step had trodden black.
Oh, I kept the first for another day!

Giving these lines and the title their due, the poem's theme seems to be that making any choice necessarily excludes the other options, and therefore involves loss. The speaker's "sigh" is for the road not taken – the alternative course, the alternate life, that was once a possibility but is now gone for good, simply because "way leads on to way". To some extent, the poem's sense depends on whether the reader hears regret or pride in the tone of the final stanza – both are possible, but choosing either, insisting on one to the exclusion of the other, involves a loss.

Frost recorded a statement on where and when this poem was written, and the circumstances that prompted its composition. Elliott Baker, in his memoir of Frost, tells how he filmed Frost reading this poem for use on television. Frost said he needed to warm up before reciting the poem, and Baker suggested he say something about the writing of the poem and its inspiration. What Frost then said was filmed and recorded:

> In 1914 we were in this farmhouse in Gloucestershire, in England. It was summer, but we needed a log fire some nights. And we were sitting around this big, open fireplace, my friend Edward Thomas and his wife Helen and Elinor and me, and it was right after we'd heard that war'd been declared. Edward thought he should join up right away and then he thought maybe he'd better wait a little. He was always like that when he had a decision to make, weighing this and that, looking one way and another for a long time before choosing what he'd do. So the poem came less from me than from him.

Frost spoke of Thomas as if they were spiritual brothers, able to confide wholeheartedly in each other. Both had married and started families relatively young. Both had financial difficulties. Both loved the outdoors, and solitude, and suffered from bouts of depression. It is often said that Frost encouraged Thomas to be a poet by showing him how excerpts from his prose might stand as poems if they were rearranged to appear on the page as verse. If so, Thomas more than returned the favour by providing the basis for 'The Road Not Taken'.

'Birches' is one of a series of poems that includes 'The Tuft of Flowers' and 'The Wood-pile'. In each of these poems a first-person narrator, in effect the poet (although Frost's statement on the source for 'The Road Not Taken' indicates the need to be careful about such identifications), makes a discovery while outdoors, and reflections on that discovery lead to a revelation, an increase in self-awareness.

The poem consists of 59 lines of blank verse organised into four sections. In this case, the poem opens with the physical sight that is the discovery that propels thought:

> When I see birches bend to left and right
> Across the lines of straighter darker trees,
> I like to think some boy's been swinging them.

This straightforward beginning is interrupted by a long diversion, a consideration of an alternative cause of the bending birches, an ice storm. This diversion is an imaginative description that combines accurate observation with strong writing:

> Often you must have seen them
> Loaded with ice a sunny winter morning
> After a rain. They click upon themselves
> As the breeze rises, and turn many-colored
> As the stir cracks and crazes their enamel.

This section ends with one of Frost's most breathtaking similes, a simile that introduces an erotic element into the poem:

> You may see their trunks arching in the woods
> Years afterwards, trailing their leaves on the ground
> Like girls on hands and knees that throw their hair
> Before them over their heads to dry in the sun.

To break the spell of this vision, Frost goes back to his original thought that a boy had bent the birches by swinging them:

> But I was going to say when Truth broke in
> With all her matter of fact about the ice-storm
> I should prefer to have some boy bend them
> As he went out and in to fetch the cows –

It is, of course, funny that the narrator describes all the metaphoric and alliterative language expended on the ice storm as "matter of fact". If anything, the description of the boy swinging birches is more matter-of-fact, although it is of course possible to read this section as metaphoric too, possibly as a metaphor for how Frost pursued his career:

> He learned all there was
> To learn about not launching out too soon
> And so not carrying the tree away
> Clear to the ground. He always kept his poise
> To the top branches, climbing carefully
> With the same pains you use to fill a cup
> Up to the brim, and even above the brim.

The erotic element in this section is not concerned with the opposite sex, but rather with generational rivalries between father and son, with the son outstripping the father:

> One by one he subdued his father's trees
> By riding them down over and over again
> Until he took the stiffness out of them,
> And not one but hung limp, not one was left
> For him to conquer.

In the fourth and final section of the poem, the speaker identifies himself with the boy: "So was I once myself a swinger of birches./ And so I dream of going back to be."

This identification of the speaker with the boy allows for the serious subject of the poem to emerge. The speaker is lost and confused, and indulges in the wish to leave the world awhile and then return to it and start over. This description of a spiritual condition, a spiritual condition caused by the way love has been going for the speaker, is in terms of Frost's trek through the Dismal Swamp and in terms that connect this poem with 'The Road Not Taken' despite their obvious differences:

> It's when I'm weary of considerations,
> And life is too much like a pathless wood
> Where your face burns and tickles with the cobwebs
> Broken across it, and one eye is weeping
> From a twig's having lashed across it open.
> I'd like to get away from earth awhile
> And then come back to it and begin over.

As this passage suggests, Frost's best poems arise as "momentary stays against confusion," as he said in 'The Figure A Poem Makes', defences of words he erected when he felt overwhelmed. This fear of being overwhelmed seems to be related to guilt, depression, and physical ailments that frequently bedevilled him, all of which were often related to the life he shared with his wife and children. The speaker of this poem makes clear that his wish to leave the earth is not a death wish, but rather a wish to be refreshed and renewed by returning to an act of boyhood that predates sexuality, marriage, family, and career, adult responsibilities:

> I'd like to go by climbing a birch tree,
> And climb black branches up a snow-white trunk
> *Toward* heaven, till the tree could bear no more,
> But dipped its top and set me down again.

While this poem at root is dark, little of that darkness remains with the reader. The memory of it is marked mostly by delight and even a sense of innocence. The understatement of the poem's concluding line seems to endorse, in an offhand way, the adult male's dream of escape: "One could do worse than be a swinger of birches". Frost once said that there are two kinds of realists. The first kind offers you a potato with the dirt still on it to prove it is a potato. The other kind offers you a clean potato. He said he was the second kind of realist, and he could have had 'Birches' in mind when he said it.

Some of the less well-known poems in *Mountain Interval* are as good as, if not better than, the famous ones. Compared to 'Birches', 'An Old Man's Winter Night' is a potato with plenty of dirt still on it. Instead of remembering his boyhood and wishing to relive it, Frost in this poem imagines a lonely old age, not overtly for himself, but for a character, the old man of the poem's title. There is a soft-spoken urgency to the poem that suggests it came the way Frost said poems should: "Like a piece of ice on a hot stove the poem must ride on its own melting":

> All out-of-doors looked darkly in at him
> Through the thin frost, almost in separate stars,
> That gathers on the pane in empty rooms.

The immediate reference to the frost, combined with Frost's propensity for punning on his name, almost defines the point-of-view of this poem-objective, because there is no use of a first-person narrator here – yet personal, as if a likeness of the old man is caught in the mirror of Frost's temperament, personality.

Nothing to speak of happens in the poem. It is no narrative of discovery like 'Birches'. Instead, the old man sits at a table, having stomped around the empty house, and then sleeps. In a way, the discovery in this poem is acceptance of, resignation to, the idea that human discoveries are of no use, are insufficient in themselves, and so must be supplemented with reliance on a higher power. In this case, the moon represents that higher power, and the old man's willingness to rely on her is expressed in the form of a slightly ironic prayer – a slightly ironic prayer whose imagery suggests this poem might owe something to a poem that must have meant much to Frost, Coleridge's 'Frost at Midnight':

> He consigned to the moon – such as she was,
> So late-arising – to the broken moon,
> As better than the sun in any case
> For such a charge, his snow upon the roof,
> His icicles along the wall to keep;
> And slept.

Frost is often thought of as an advocate of self-reliance and individualism – and he was, in talks, in prose, when he put his faith in the masculine sun of rationalism, his father's path. But in poems – or, better, in this poem – he certainly recognised the severe limits of self-reliance and individualism:

> One aged man – one man – can't keep a house,
> A farm, a countryside, or if he can,
> It's thus he does it of a winter night.

In this poem, the price of self-reliance, individualism, is a loneliness that is so confining it is claustrophobic and seems to threaten madness. The sounds of the "outer night" are said to be more like "the beating on a box" than anything else. If it is legitimate to see a poem such as this one as commenting on the human condition, that condition consists of being alone, weak, and tired in a threatening environment, with only the "broken moon" to turn to for help.

The first poem in Frost's first book was a sonnet in which the poet played with the form – a practice of Frost's throughout his whole career. In *Mountain Interval,* 'The Oven Bird' is such a sonnet and Frost seems to have used it here to look at how he then stood as a poet. The sonnet opens the way a Shakespearean sonnet traditionally closes, with a couplet:

> There is a singer everyone has heard,
> Loud, a mid-summer and a mid-wood bird,
> Who makes the solid tree trunks sound again.

Frost said poems should begin in delight and end in wisdom. The rhythm of these opening lines, even more than what they say, shows the delight with which Frost began writing this poem.

He next makes a series of three statements on what the bird 'says' when it makes "the solid tree trunks sound again". It is well to remember that Frost always insisted that he 'said' his poems when he read them aloud or recited them publicly. The repetitive use of the phrase "he says" of the oven bird serves to identify the bird with the poet. In a way, what the bird does and this poem itself are both examples of Frost's theory of the sentence as a sound with a sense apart from the meanings of the words that make it up. That theory is behind the poem's turning toward wisdom in the end:

> The bird would cease and be as other birds
> But that he knows in singing not to sing.
> The question that he frames in all but words
> Is what to make of a diminished thing.

What is sometimes called 'organic form' in poetry simply means that the content and the form of a poem are, or should be, one, inseparable, the shape of the thing supporting or echoing its substance. The variations in the traditional sonnet form in this poem help to define the poem's subject, the oven bird, as a singer who says but does not sing, a paradox perfectly reflected in the poem's playful, paradoxical form. Similarly, the poem's rhythm goes from the assertive, almost rollicking opening lines to the sad clarity of its conclusion. It seems to be the case that Frost realised with the publication of *Mountain Interval* that his poetic gift had become "a diminished thing."

Signs of this diminished gift are present in the book. 'In the Home Stretch' is a long narrative, a dialogue between a man and wife of the kind that dominates *North of Boston.* The title of the poem and an element of its plot – the husband insists on knowing what the wife sees when she looks out a window – call for the reader to compare this poem with 'Home Burial'. 'In the Home Stretch' cannot survive such a comparison – it has nothing of the earlier poem's power. In part this is no doubt because it is a happier poem, dealing with a couple moving into a new home rather than with a couple grieving the death of a first child. Still, 'In the Home Stretch' is diffuse and verbose in a way 'Home Burial' is not.

Another poem in *Mountain Interval* that shows the diminishment of Frost's gift is 'Out, Out ' a title that alludes to a speech in Shakespeare's *Macbeth* that refers to a haunting sense of guilt following a murder. Neither this allusion nor the poem's 34 lines of blank verse do justice to the poem's subject, an accidental loss of a hand by a boy using a buzz saw that leads to the boy's death. The poem's conclusion:

> And they, since they
> Were not the one dead, turned to their affairs.

seems to share the cruel indifference of the people it discusses. It is this lack of emotion, involvement, that gives the poem an artificial, worked up feel.

In 1915, the year before *Mountain Interval* appeared, Frost read some of its contents, including 'The Road Not Taken' and 'Birches', at Tufts, a university, near Boston. The pleasure he took in this public reading seems to have suggested to him what he might make of the diminished thing of his poetic gift. Throughout the rest of his career, Frost would devote a good deal of his time and energy to touring the country to read his work.

4

Barding About: The Later Poems

There is an unforgettable television image of Robert Frost reading at the inauguration of a President of the United States, John F. Kennedy, on 20th January 1961. The old man's white hair lifts in the breeze as he tries in vain to read a poem he has composed for the occasion, a poem that is meant to lead into – introduce his reading of 'The Gift Outright'. Blinded by the glare of the sun, the aged poet in the end gives up and recites from memory 'The Gift Outright', a poem he has altered slightly at the request of the new president. This moment no doubt represents the height of one aspect of Frost's career, the aspect Frost himself referred to as "barding about".

What he meant by "barding about" was travelling the country, giving readings and talks, at times teaching, at times being a poet in residence at one college campus or another, and in general earning a living from the fees for these activities while building the audience for his books of poems. Frost pursued the opportunity to read his poems in public compulsively just as he had once been compelled to write poems. The fact is that publicly reading his work hindered his ability to write it or, at least, accompanied a decline in his ability to write it. He once confessed in a letter to Louis Untermeyer that he was now confined to taking to market the poems he had written as a relatively young man. This statement was an exaggeration, but it also included more than a little truth.

He published no book of poems between 1916, when *Mountain Interval* appeared, and 1923, when he was almost fifty years old. This seven-year period was marked by public success and private woes and worries. He won prizes, was paid well for readings and talks, held various academic posts, and was awarded numerous honorary degrees. On the other hand, Edward Thomas was killed in France in 1917, deeply affecting Frost. In 1920, Frost's sister, Jeanie, was pronounced insane and Frost committed her to a state mental hospital in Augusta, Maine, necessarily renewing Frost's own fears of the possibility of an inherited streak of madness.

When Frost published two books in 1923, his first *Selected Poems,* and then a new volume of verse, *New Hampshire,* it was immediately clear his fame had grown. The books sold exceedingly well; and for *New Hampshire* Frost was awarded the first of the four Pulitzer Prizes he would receive in his lifetime. The volume also made it clear that something had gone very wrong with Frost as a poet. *New Hampshire* is the first of Frost's books to be illustrated with woodcuts by J.J. Lankes. There is not, of course, anything in itself wrong with this. It just shows a shift from plain texts to a 'package' designed with an eye to the market, a market that wants simplicity and quaintness in the aftermath of the First World War and the Russian Revolution, and in the midst of the roaring twenties, the Jazz Age. Worse, that market had been developed by Frost's recitals and talks, his public appearances, and these tended to feature Frost as a craggy but genial Yankee Farmer, a cross between Santa Claus and Ralph Waldo Emerson, a part Frost played well, but a part all the same. The deadly aspect of this public role surfaces when, in the title poem of *New Hampshire,* the first-person narrator of the poem is this character rather than the first person narrator of 'Mending Wall'. On the page, rather than in the auditorium or on the lecture circuit, this character comes across as the real Frost's ventriloquist's dummy, at once shallow and coy, a self-parody:

> I choose to be a plain New Hampshire farmer
> With an income in cash of, say, a thousand
> (From, say, a publisher in New York City).
> It's restful to arrive at a decision,
> And restful just to think about New Hampshire.
> At present I am living in Vermont.

It is painful to think of the man who wrote 'Home Burial' setting down these lines of pop icon chatter and sending them off to his publisher in New York City. The good news is that not all of the poems in the book are like this one.

The volume *New Hampshire* also includes one of Frost's best-known poems, 'Stopping by Woods on a Snowy Evening'. The first-person narrator of this famous poem has much more in common with the narrator of 'Mending Wall' or 'Birches' than with the narrator of 'New Hampshire'. This narrator is in a familiar setting, is at home, yet makes a discovery of sorts – a slight discovery, perhaps, but a discovery all the same. It is the kind of discovery Frost described in his 'The Figure A Poem Makes' " ... not necessarily a great clarification, such as sects and cults are founded on, but ... a momentary stay against confusion".

The source of the confusion clarified in 'Stopping by Woods on a Snowy Evening' is the contradictory impulse to at once stop and go on. The horse, rather than the speaker of the poem, is the advocate of going:

> He gives his harness bells a shake
> To ask if there is some mistake.
> The only other sound's the sweep
> Of easy wind and downy flake.

The narrator, on the other hand, expresses the wish to "watch his woods fill up with snow", that is, to take pleasure in a natural phenomenon that causes an arresting beauty. The conflict at the heart of this poem might be a metaphor for the conflict between poetry – sitting and staring – and duty, the routine, habitual round of a beast of burden with the narrator's "promises to keep". In a way, the conflict for Frost was between "barding about" and patiently waiting for poems like those in *North of Boston* to come to him. The resolution of this conflict is a compromise, a postponement of the demands of duty in order to participate briefly in poetry. The act of writing the poem is the resolution of the conflict the poem contains.

The wide appeal of this poem no doubt rests on its daydream-like wish for relief from the dull round of duty combined with the simplicity of the poem's rhymes and the song-like quality of its rhythm. On the other hand, these traits constitute a weakness in the poem, the readiness with which it can be – and has been – parodied. The inversion in the first line – "Whose woods these are I think I know" rather than "I think I know whose woods these are" can be defended on the ground that it emphasises the woods rather than the speaker, but it nonetheless is necessary for the rhyme scheme of the first stanza. As a result, it comes across as a mannerism rather than a manner, a hook for the parodists. Whose words these are I think I know. Worse, the lazy adjectives "easy" and "downy" are used to pad out a line's metre. In that same stanza, an inconsistent use of contractions ("there is" but "sound's") to fit the metre shows an unwillingness on the poet's part to let the poem find its own form. But what really made the poem a target for the parodist and the recipient of contempt was its sheer popularity, its success with audiences, the way it jingled in the mind of the public like the bells of the horse's harness from Frost's repeated readings of it, often by popular demand. 'Stopping by Woods on a Snowy Evening' is the verbal equivalent of Frost's public persona. It is a tour de force that involves a simplification that falsifies.

"The poet in me died nearly ten years ago," Frost wrote to Louis Untermeyer on 4th May 1916. "Fortunately he had run through several phases, four to be exact, all well-defined, before he went. The calf I was in the nineties I merely take to market. I am become my own salesman." This statement is marked by an honesty that demands it be taken seriously. It does not mean that Frost stopped writing poems in 1907 or so unless we take care with the use of the word poem. Frost could virtually always write things like 'New Hampshire'. The question is whether or not they deserve the name poem. Frost did not think so.

He famously said that a poem "could never be a put-up job". He insisted that a poem started with "a lump in the throat", a lump in the throat that arose from "homesickness" or "lovesickness". He was well aware that not all of the verses he wrote and published sprang from such a source. Rather, he also wrote verses when there was no lump in his throat because he had the wish to write a poem, or keep his name before the public, or take part in his country's cultural life. In other words, he tried to will the things into being when he was not compelled to give them life.

Frost's reference to his early death as a poet (in 1906 he published 'A Tuft of Flowers' and took a job as a teacher, perhaps turning slightly away from the 'poetic' life he had shared with Elinor and their children on the farm near Derry, New Hampshire) does not mean that no real poems by him appeared throughout the rest of his long life. Instead, it means that he always held some relatively early poems back and published them later, sometimes in a revised form. It also means that from time to time he wrote additional poems that started as a lump in his throat. It is just that these poems came less and less frequently, and not in a concentrated rush as they had when he lived on the farm near Derry.

'Design' is one of those poems Frost held back from publication for years. It was originally entitled 'In White', and was already in existence by 1912. The poem was first collected in the volume entitled *A Further Range,* published in 1936, a Book-of-the-Month Club selection that was awarded the Pulitzer Prize. The main differences brought about by the revision of the poem are that it now opens with a first-person narrator ("I found a dimpled spider, fat and white"), and that some archaic melodramatic language was excised. For instance, the sonnet's concluding couplet read:

> What but design of darkness and of night?
> Design, design! Do I use the word aright?

but became in the published version:

> What but design of darkness to appall? –
> If design govern in a thing so small.

On the other hand, there were times when poems that deserve that name still came to him. Frost's wife died in 1938. Later that year, he fell in love with a younger, married woman, Kathleen Morrison, and asked her to marry him. She refused to do so, but agreed to become his paid assistant and secretary. He dedicated the volume entitled *A Witness Tree,* published in 1942, to her. It contains a love sonnet, 'The Silken Tent', that shows that if the poet in Frost died in about 1906 he was capable of resurrection in 1938. The sonnet is a single, breath-taking sentence with a sublimated erotic charge to it:

> She is as in a field a silken tent
> At midday when a sunny summer breeze
> Has dried the dew and all its ropes relent,
> So that in guys it gently sways at ease.

The work contains for readers that sense of surprise that Frost insisted could only be communicated if it had first been experienced by the poet – in this case, the surprise of falling in love late in life.

There are other poems that might have been written or begun early and were then held back, left unharvested for decades, or might have been written later. It is difficult to tell. Two such poems are 'Too Anxious for Rivers' and 'The Directive'. They were first collected in *Steeple Bush,* a volume published in 1947. Both poems are distinguished by their imaginative diction – diction that is not only modern but, for Frost, surprisingly modernistic. The subjects of these poems, as well as their language, suggest that they are relatively late. 'Too Anxious for Rivers' reads in part:

> It may be a mercy the dark closes round us
> So broodingly soon in every direction.
> The world as we know is an elephant's howdah;
> The elephant stands on the back of a turtle;
> The turtle in turn on a rock in the ocean.
> And how much longer a story has science
> Before she must put out the light on the children
> And tell them the rest of the story is dreaming?

Although 'Too Anxious for Rivers' has something of the serious whimsy of 'The Mountain', this poem stands apart from the mainstream of Frost's work.

'Directive', on the other hand, has clear affinities with some of Frost's early poems. It is another one of those longish narratives of discovery like 'The Tuft of Flowers', 'Birches', and 'The Wood-pile'. The speaker of 'Directive', though, urges the reader to make the discovery rather than reporting on having done so himself:

> Back out of all this now too much for us,
> Back in a time made simple by the loss
> Of detail, burned, dissolved, and broken off
> Like graveyard marble sculpture in the weather,
> There is a house that is no more a house
> Upon a farm that is no more a farm
> And in a town that is no more a town.

This specific, but riddling, scene ties the poem to very early work. The poem 'Ghost House', published in *A Boy's Will*, Frost's first book, begins:

> I dwell in a lonely house I know
> That vanished many a summer ago,
> And left no trace but the cellar walls,
> And a cellar in which the daylight falls
> And the purple-stemmed wild raspberries grow.

In 'The Generations of Men', a poem in *North of Boston* that celebrates the beginning of a relationship between a man and a woman when a family reunion is rained out, the scene is an old family farm described in terms that are reminiscent of both 'Ghost House' and the scene of 'Directive':

> "One ought not to be thrown into confusion
> By a plain statement of relationship,
> But I own what you say makes my head spin.
> You take my card – you seem so good at such things –
> And see if you can reckon our cousinship.
> Why not take seats here on the cellar wall
> And dangle feet among the raspberry vines?"

Finally, the scene set in 'Directive' is also reminiscent of the marble gravestones Amy stares at through the window in 'Home Burial'.

It seems likely that Frost's father's family home in Lawrence, Massachusetts, the home his mother took him to as a child, the home where his mother, his father, and his son Elliott were buried, served as the basis of this repetitive scene, a scene that took on mythic proportions for him, a scene he associated with fundamental sources of confusion about love, death, and identity. It was this source of confusion, related as it was to both homesickness and love-sickness, that gave rise to the lump in the throat that signalled for Frost the coming of a poem, the kind of poem that is worthy of that name. Here is the magical ending of 'Directive':

> I have kept hidden in the instep arch
> Of an old cedar at the waterside
> A broken drinking goblet like the Grail
> Under a spell so the wrong ones can't find it,
> So can't get saved, as Saint Mark says they mustn't.
> (I stole the goblet from the children's playhouse.)
> Here are your waters and your watering place.
> Drink and be whole again beyond confusion.

A poem such as this one has little or nothing to do with Robert Frost, the showman, who went barding about the country and ultimately became a public figure who took part in a presidential inauguration. It has much more to do with a youngish man, a husband and father, sitting up late at night on a farm in New Hampshire, suffering from a longing he could never fully understand, but that he found he could temporarily exorcise with the rapid movement of a pen.

Afterword

Lionel Trilling, the critic, spoke at a dinner held at the Waldorf-Astoria Hotel in New York in 1959 to celebrate Frost's 85th birthday. Trilling attacked the public image of Frost to try and get at the truth of him, the truth of his work.

He told his audience that the Frost he found in the work was very different from the Frost "I seem to perceive existing in the minds of so many of his admirers ... He is not the Frost who reassures us by his affirmation of old virtues, simplicities, pieties, and ways of feeling: anything but." Trilling concluded that Frost was a "terrifying" – or tragic – poet, a poet who "conceives a terrifying universe" that is inhabited by people who lead terrible, terrifying lives: " ... whenever have people been so isolated, so lightning-blasted, so tied down and calcined by life, so reduced, each in his own way, to some last irreducible core of being." He also argued that Frost's work was peculiarly American because it shared with the classics of American literature what D.H. Lawrence found in them – a voice that was engaged in shedding the consciousness of Europe and coaxing a new consciousness into being.

This dose gave some of the attendees of the dinner intellectual indigestion. Frost himself, who had to get up and read after Trilling had finished, had been clearly shaken by the critic's comments, by his having been taken seriously in public. He wanted to grin slyly and joke with people: he didn't want to terrify anyone. In the days and weeks that followed the celebration, a literary debate took place in which some of Frost's admirers attacked Trilling.

The terrifying, the tragic element in Frost's work had been there from the start. The wonder is that it could have been so thoroughly missed, suppressed and ignored, for decades. Frost's understandable unwillingness or inability to read 'Home Burial' in public shows one of the reasons it was missed – the terrifying aspect of his work was not suitable for public performance. Another reason, of course, is that the race is not anxious to face the terrifying and so looks the other way.

After Frost's death, his official biographer, the biographer Frost had selected himself, Lawrance Thompson, completed two of three projected volumes of a life of Frost. (One of Thompson's students finished the third volume after Thompson's death.) Thompson, who had once admired, perhaps idolised, Frost, became disillusioned with him. Critics were shocked by the Frost Thompson depicted – ambitious, petty, vain, malicious, competitive, arrogant, and so on. Thompson did for Frost's life what Trilling had done for his work: freed it from the public image so it could be re-evaluated. Those people who have come to think of Frost as a nasty man who wrote terrifying poems are probably as far from the mark as those who thought of him as an avuncular duffer who wrote quaint lyrics. He was a man, not a caricature – not even the caricature of his own making, the stage Yankee with the craggy brows.

Frost's public life seems to have been an attempted escape from a sad private life and his own insecurities. The death of his first son and the insanity of his sister established early the dominant tone of his family life. Frost used to complain that people thought he was cruel or indifferent just because he refused to die when other people died or to go insane when other people had gone insane. As poor health, mental instability, and suicide stalked his family, Frost accumulated real estate, drove hard bargains with his publisher, collected prizes and honorary degrees, and continued an all but constant round of readings and academic appointments. There is a sense that he was not as good at what meant most to him – being a husband and a father – than he was at charming strangers, acquaintances, and colleagues.

One of Frost's best poems, 'Acquainted With the Night', first collected in *West-Running Brook,* published in 1928, reflects the isolation that was at the root of both the public and the private Frost. This sense of isolation is conveyed by the poem's form and rhythm as much as by what it says.

Frost experimented with the sonnet form throughout his life. 'Acquainted With the Night' is a sonnet in a form associated with Dante, the author of *The Divine Comedy.* Frost's sonnet consists of four three-line stanzas of *terza rima,* followed by a couplet. This form is tightly bound together by interlocking rhymes, giving the poem a slightly claustrophobic feel, a feel reinforced by the poem's last line repeating its first, "I have been one acquainted with the night". This repetition of the first line as the last makes this sonnet a refutation of the idea of progress in 14 lines. It ends where it began – and threatens to begin all over again, following the same course, the words on the page echoing the footsteps of the speaker:

> I have stood still and stopped the sound of feet
> When far away an interrupted cry
> Came over houses from another street,
>
> But not to call me back or say good-bye;

The repeated use of the first-person singular at the beginning of lines serves to emphasise the loneliness, the isolation of the speaker:

> I have been one acquainted with the night.
> I have walked out in rain – and back in rain.
> I have out-walked the furthest city light.

Ending each of these lines with a full-stop gives the sense that the speaker is trapped, as if pacing a room or a cell.

'Acquainted With the Night' might have been one of those poems by Frost in which the speaker reports on a walk which led to a discovery. An almost surrealistic image seems to at once offer and deny the possibility of making a discovery:

> And further still at an unearthly height
> One luminary clock against the sky
>
> Proclaimed the time was neither wrong nor right.

This inability to make a discovery, the repetition of the first line as the last, and the use of a form associated with Dante all suggest that the speaker of this poem is one of the dead or the damned, the living dead. It is perhaps the confession of the poet in Frost, the poet he frankly admitted had died early. If so, it is further evidence of the kind of poet he was, the kind for whom a poem could never be "a put-up job".

Selected Bibliography

Books by Robert Frost

A Boy's Will (London, 1913; New York, 1915)

North of Boston (London, 1914; New York, 1915)

Mountain Interval (New York, 1916)

Selected Poems (New York, 1923)

New Hampshire (New York, 1923)

West-Running Brook (New York, 1928)

Collected Poems (New York, 1930)

A Further Range (New York, 1936)

A Witness Tree (New York, 1942)

Steeple Bush (New York, 1947)

Complete Poems of Robert Frost 1949 (New York, 1949)

In The Clearing (New York, 1962)

Louis Untermeyer, ed. *The Letters of Robert Frost to Louis Untermeyer* (New York, 1963)

Lawrance Thompson, ed. *Selected Letters of Robert Frost* (New York, 1964)

Richard Poirier and Mark Richardson, eds. *Robert Frost: Collected Poems,Prose, and Plays* (New York: The Library of America, 1995)

Note: The publisher of Frost's early books in London was David Nutt and Co. Frost's New York publisher was Henry Holt and Co.

Works on Robert Frost

Baker, Elliott, *Confectionaries* (Philadelphia: Xlibris, 2003)

Burnshaw, Stanley, *Robert Frost Himself* (New York: Holt, Rhinehart, and Winston, 1976)

Parini, Jay, *Robert Frost: A Life* (New York: Henry Holt & Company, 1999)

Thompson, Lawrance, *Robert Frost: The Early Years, 1874-1915* (New York: Holt, Rhinehart and Winston, 1966)

Thompson, Lawrance, *Robert Frost: The Years of Triumph, 1915-1938* (New York: Holt, Rhinehart and Winston, 1970)

Thompson, Lawrance, and R.H. Winnick, *Robert Frost: The Later Years, 1938-1963* (New York: Holt, Rhinehart and Winston, 1976)

Trilling, Lionel, 'A Speech on Robert Frost: A Cultural Episode', *Partisan Review,* Summer 1959

GREENWICH EXCHANGE BOOKS

Greenwich Exchange Student Guides are critical studies of major or contemporary serious writers in English and selected European languages. The series is for the student, the teacher and 'common readers' and is an ideal resource for libraries. The *Times Educational Supplement* praised these books, saying, "The style of these guides has a pressure of meaning behind it. Students should learn from that ... If art is about selection, perception and taste, then this is it."

(ISBN prefix 1-871551- applies)

The series includes:
W.H. Auden by Stephen Wade (36-6)
Honoré de Balzac by Wendy Mercer (48-X)
William Blake by Peter Davies (27-7)
The Brontës by Peter Davies (24-2)
Robert Browning by John Lucas (59-5)
Samuel Taylor Coleridge by Andrew Keanie (64-1)
Joseph Conrad by Martin Seymour-Smith (18-8)
William Cowper by Michael Thorn (25-0)
Charles Dickens by Robert Giddings (26-9)
Emily Dickinson by Marnie Pomeroy (68-4)
John Donne by Sean Haldane (23-4)
Ford Madox Ford by Anthony Fowles (63-3)
Thomas Hardy by Sean Haldane (35-1)
Seamus Heaney by Warren Hope (37-4)
Philip Larkin by Warren Hope (35-8)
Philip Roth by Paul McDonald (72-2)
Shakespeare's Non-Dramatic Poetry by Martin Seymour-Smith (22-6)
Shakespeare's *Macbeth* by Matt Simpson (69-2)
Shakespeare's *Othello* by Matt Simpson (71-4)
Shakespeare's Sonnets by Martin Seymour-Smith (38-2)
Tobias Smollett by Robert Giddings (21-8)
Alfred, Lord Tennyson by Michael Thorn (20-X)
The Plays of Joe Orton by Arthur Burke (56-0)
William Wordsworth by Andrew Keanie (57-9)

OTHER GREENWICH EXCHANGE BOOKS
Paperback unless otherwise stated.

LITERURE AND BIOGRAPHY

The Author, the Book and the Reader
Robert Giddings
This collection of essays analyses the effects of changing technology and the attendant commercial pressures on literary styles and subject matter. Authors covered include Charles Dickens, Tobias George Smollett, Mark Twain, Dr Johnson and John le Carré.
1991 • 220 pages • illustrated • ISBN 1-871551-01-3

John Dryden
Anthony Fowles
Of all the poets of the Augustan age, John Dryden was the most worldly. Anthony Fowles traces Dryden's evolution from 'wordsmith' to major poet.
This critical study shows a poet of vigour and technical panache whose art was forged in the heat and battle of a turbulent polemical and pamphleteering age. Although Dryden's status as a literary critic has long been established, Fowles draws attention to Dryden's neglected achievements as a translator of poetry. He deals also with the less well-known aspects of Dryden's work – his plays and occasional pieces.
Born in London and educated at the Universities of Oxford and Southern California, Anthony Fowles began his career in filmmaking before becoming an author of film and television scrips and more than twenty books. Readers will welcome the many contemporary references to novels and film with which Fowles illuminates the life and work of this decisively influential English poetic voice.

The Good That We Do
John Lucas
John Lucas' book blends fiction, biography and social history in order to tell the story of his grandfather, Horace Kelly. Headteacher of a succession of elementary schools in impoverished areas of London, 'Hod' Kelly was also a keen cricketer, a devotee of the music hall, and included among his friends the great Trade Union leader, Ernest Bevin. In telling the story of his life, Lucas has provided a fascinating range of insights into the lives of ordinary Londoners from the First World War until the outbreak of the Second World War. Threaded throughout is an account of such people's hunger for education, and of the different ways government, church and

educational officialdom ministered to that hunger. *The Good That We Do* is both a study of one man and of a period when England changed, drastically and forever.

John Lucas is Professor of English at Nottingham Trent University and is a poet and critic.

2001 • 214 pages • ISBN 1-871551-54-4

In Pursuit of Lewis Carroll

Raphael Shaberman

Sherlock Holmes and the author uncover new evidence in their investigations into the mysterious life and writing of Lewis Carroll. They examine published works by Carroll that have been overlooked by previous commentators. A newly discovered poem, almost certainly by Carroll, is published here.

Amongst many aspects of Carroll's highly complex personality, this book explores his relationship with his parents, numerous child friends, and the formidable Mrs Liddell, mother of the immortal Alice. Raphael Shaberman was a founder member of the Lewis Carroll Society and a teacher of autistic children.

1994 • 118 pages • illustrated • ISBN 1-871551-13-7

Liar! Liar!: Jack Kerouac – Novelist

R.J. Ellis

The fullest study of Jack Kerouac's fiction to date. It is the first book to devote an individual chapter to every one of his novels. *On the Road, Visions of Cody* and *The Subterraneans* are reread in-depth, in a new and exciting way. *Visions of Gerard* and *Doctor Sax* are also strikingly reinterpreted, as are other daringly innovative writings, like 'The Railroad Earth' and his "try at a spontaneous *Finnegan's Wake*" – *Old Angel Midnight*. Neglected writings, such as *Tristessa* and *Big Sur*, are also analysed, alongside better-known novels such as *Dharma Bums* and *Desolation Angels*.

R.J. Ellis is Senior Lecturer in English at Nottingham Trent University.

1999 • 295 pages • ISBN 1-871551-53-6

Musical Offering

Yolanthe Leigh

In a series of vivid sketches, anecdotes and reflections, Yolanthe Leigh tells the story of her growing up in the Poland of the 30s and the Second World War. These are poignant episodes of a child's first encounters with both the enchantments and the cruelties of the world; and from a later time, stark memories of the brutality of the Nazi invasion, and the hardships of student life in Warsaw under the Occupation. But most of all this is a record of inward development; passages of remarkable intensity and simplicity describe the girl's response to religion, to music, and to her discovery of philosophy.

Yolanthe Leigh was formerly a Lecturer in Philosophy at Reading University.

2000 • 57 pages • ISBN: 1-871551-46-3

Norman Cameron

Warren Hope

Norman Cameron's poetry was admired by W.H. Auden, celebrated by Dylan Thomas and valued by Robert Graves. He was described by Martin Seymour-Smith as, "one of … the most rewarding and pure poets of his generation …" and is at last given a full length biography. This eminently sociable man, who had periods of darkness and despair, wrote little poetry by comparison with others of his time, but always of a consistently high quality – imaginative and profound.

2000 • 221 pages • illustrated • ISBN 1-871551-05-6

POETRY

Adam's Thoughts in Winter

Warren Hope

Warren Hope's poems have appeared from time to time in a number of literary periodicals, pamphlets and anthologies on both sides of the Atlantic. They appeal to lovers of poetry everywhere. His poems are brief, clear, frequently lyrical, characterised by wit, but often distinguished by tenderness. The poems gathered in this first book-length collection counter the brutalising ethos of contemporary life, speaking of and for the virtues of modesty, honesty and gentleness in an individual, memorable way.

2000 • 47 pages • ISBN 1-871551-40-4

Baudelaire: Les Fleurs du Mal

Translated by F.W. Leakey

Selected poems from *Les Fleurs du Mal* are translated with parallel French texts and are designed to be read with pleasure by readers who have no French as well as those who are practised in the French language.

F.W. Leakey was Professor of French in the University of London. As a scholar, critic and teacher he specialised in the work of Baudelaire for 50 years and published a number of books on the poet.

2001 • 153 pages • ISBN 1-871551-10-2

Lines from the Stone Age
Sean Haldane
Reviewing Sean Haldane's 1992 volume *Desire in Belfast*, Robert Nye wrote in *The Times* that "Haldane can be sure of his place among the English poets." This place is not yet a conspicuous one, mainly because his early volumes appeared in Canada and because he has earned his living by other means than literature. Despite this, his poems have always had their circle of readers. The 60 previously unpublished poems of *Lines from the Stone Age* – "lines of longing, terror, pride, lust and pain" – may widen this circle.
2000 • 53 pages • ISBN 1-871551-39-0

Wilderness
Martin Seymour-Smith
This is Martin Seymour-Smith's first publication of his poetry for more than twenty years. This collection of 36 poems is a fearless account of an inner life of love, frustration, guilt, laughter and the celebration of others. He is best known to the general public as the author of the controversial and bestselling *Hardy* (1994).
1994 • 52 pages • ISBN 1-871551-08-0

MISCELLANEOUS

English Language Skills
Vera Hughes
If you want to be sure, (as a student, or in your business or personal life,) that your written English is correct, this book is for you. Vera Hughes' aim is to help you remember the basic rules of spelling, grammar and punctuation. 'Noun', 'verb', 'subject', 'object' and 'adjective' are the only technical terms used. The book teaches the clear, accurate English required by the business and office world. It coaches acceptable current usage and makes the rules easier to remember.
Vera Hughes was a civil servant and is a trainer, and author of training manuals.
2002 • 142 pages • ISBN 1-871551-60-9